USBORNE

HAIR BRAIDING

USBORNE HOTSHOTS

HAIR BRAIDING

Cheryl Evans

Designed by Melissa Alaverdy

Illustrated by Chris Chaisty

*Photographs by Ray Moller
and Howard Allman*

Braiding by Cheryl Evans and Leslie Sayles

*With special thanks to Red and Kattja
Madrell, Francesca Tyler, Hannah and
Emily Kirby-Jones, Amy Treppass,
Maddy York and Tom Ashby*

CONTENTS

Things you need

All you need to create these beautiful bound braids on your hair is six-stranded embroidery thread, which you can buy from sewing shops or department stores. In this book you will find out how to use it to make different patterns.

There is a huge choice of embroidery threads.

Use knitting yarns for an unusual braid.

Use subtle, toning shades, or bright, clashing threads.

Rainbow knitting yarn

You can add small beads.

The threads may come in twists, like this, or straight.

Try silver or gold thread, or even thin string.

Making a holder

This simple device can be used to hold the strand of hair you are binding separate from the rest of the hair. This makes it easier to work with.

You will need: a small piece of cardboard (from a cereal box) about 7cm (3in) square; pencil; scissors.

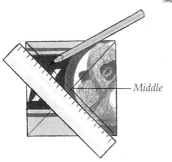

Middle

$3\frac{1}{2}$cm ($1\frac{1}{2}$in) $3\frac{1}{2}$cm ($1\frac{1}{2}$in)

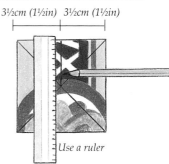

Use a ruler

1. Rule diagonal lines from the top corners of the square to the opposite corners at the bottom to find the middle of the square.

2. Place a ruler along one edge of the square and mark the middle of it ($3\frac{1}{2}$cm/$1\frac{1}{2}$in). Draw a line from this mark to the central dot.

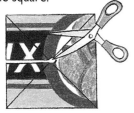

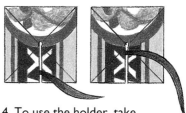

3. Cut along the line from the edge into the middle. Stick the point of the scissors in the central hole and wiggle it around to enlarge the hole.

4. To use the holder, take the strand of hair you want to braid and slide it along the slit in the cardboard and into the central hole.

Basic binding method

These steps show you the basic technique for winding embroidery thread around a strand of hair. All the other styles in this book are a variation on this method.

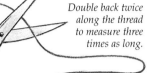

Double back twice along the thread to measure three times as long.

1. Cut a strand of embroidery thread at least three times as long as the hair you want to bind. Measure the thread along the hair.

2. Brush the hair thoroughly. Pick up a thin strand wherever on the head you want to make the braid. Slide the strand into the holder.

3. Tie the thread tightly to the top of the strand of hair with a double knot. Tie it right by the holder, which should be pushed against the head.

4. Start to wind the thread tightly around and around the strand. Wind whichever way feels easiest to you. Bind in the free, short end of thread.

5. Hold the hair stretched with one hand and wind with the other. You can help wind the thread with the fingers of the hand holding the hair.

Here you can see one braid close-up.

Bind several strands to different lengths. Tie to finish off wherever you like.

6. If spaces appear between the wound threads, push them up the hair with your finger and thumb to squeeze them together. Bind to the end.

Trim to leave short ends.

7. At the end, tie the threads around the hair and pull them tight to knot. Tie them again to make a firm double knot that will not come undone.

Two-tone braid

Now that you can do a basic braid, you can introduce
another shade of thread and start making patterns.
This two-tone braid is probably the simplest
pattern but it still looks effective.

*Trim the short ends,
if you like.*

1. Cut two lengths of different
embroidery threads about
three times as long as the hair.
Tie them together at one end.

2. Put a strand of hair in the
holder. Tie the threads to the
strand. Twist the knot so it
lies underneath the hair.

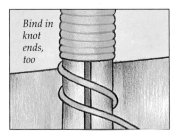

*Bind in
knot
ends,
too*

3. Lay one thread along the
strand of hair and start to
wind the other one neatly and
tightly around both the thread
and the hair.

4. After binding about 2½cm
(1in), swap the threads over,
so you now wind with the one
which was lying along the hair
and bind the first one in.

*If you want
to use one
thread more
than the
other, cut
it longer to
start with.*

5. Keep on swapping the
threads all the way down.
Vary the amounts of
each shade to get
different width stripes.
Tie a knot with both
threads at the
end of the hair.

Braids and hair care

A braid will stay in your hair for weeks if it is tightly and neatly bound and tied.

You can wash your hair carefully with the braid in.

When you want to undo a braid, carefully snip the knot at the end and unwind the threads. It takes a little time, but it's best not to just pull at it as it can get in a tangle.

Braiding can take a fairly long time, depending on how long the hair is. It can be an advantage to have shorter hair. Braids look good even on very short hair, as shown here.

Multi-shade braids

You can introduce as many different threads as you like into your braid. Experiment with threads that go with what you are wearing, or toning shades, for example.

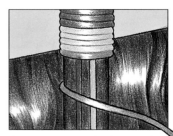

1. Put the strand of hair in the holder. Tie three threads together at one end. Tie the threads tightly around the strand of hair. Hide the knot.

2. Start binding the hair with one thread. Bind around the two other threads. Swap which thread you are binding with to use all three shades.

Timesaving tip

You cover the hair faster this way.

Cut double the length of thread. Tie the middle around the hair and wind both ends at once.

In this braid there are three shades of blue embroidery thread for a subtle, toning effect.

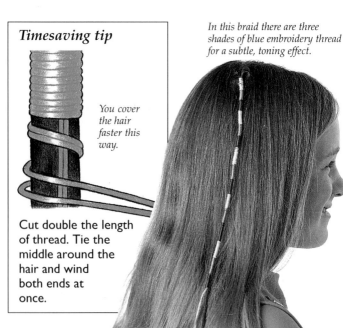

Rainbow braid

You can use as many different threads as you like. To make a rainbow, use seven threads: red, orange, yellow, green, blue, indigo (deep blue) and violet.

This is a rainbow braid.

Here are close-ups of the braids on these pages.

This is a really bright, multi-shade braid.

Spiral

Here's a different kind of pattern to add to your braids to make them more interesting. This spiral involves one thread making a pattern on top of another. It's not really difficult, you just need to plan to do it in advance.

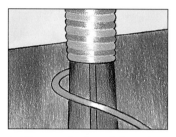

1. Tie two shades of thread onto the strand of hair and start binding neatly with whichever thread you like.

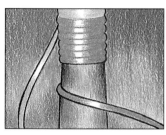

2. At some point on the braid, leave one thread out and continue binding in a solid shade for at least 4cm (1½in).

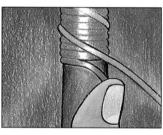

3. Wind the free thread down in a spiral on top to the end of the plain block. Hold the other thread so it doesn't unwind.

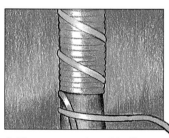

4. You can continue binding with the spiral thread, or take the other thread and bind the spiral thread in.

Variations

You can get lots of effects using the spiral technique. Use several threads, leave out two at step 2 and do a double spiral; or do a spiral over stripes.

Double spiral   *Spiral over stripes*

Space the spirals neatly and evenly down the solid block.

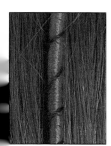

This braid shows a solid block with a single contrasting spiral on top.

Make spirals over stripes (you need three contrasting threads) for a dazzling effect.

This braid includes a two thread spiral wound over a contrasting solid block.

13

Stripes

Here's how to get even candy-stripes spiralling down
your braid. Do a completely stripy braid, or use
stripes in a pattern with larger blocks.

*Remember to have the
knot underneath so
you can bind the
ends in neatly.*

1. Put a
strand of hair in
the holder. Tightly tie on
the threads you want to use
(see alternative ideas below).

2. Bind with two strands of
different shades at the same
time. Make sure both strands
lie flat on the hair and that
they always alternate.

3. For variety, after a short
length, lay one of the threads
along the hair and continue
binding with one thread only
to make a plain block.

4. Bring out the other thread
and begin stripes again
whenever you like. Make
patterns like this to the end,
then tie a knot.

Alternative ideas

Use
three
or more
threads.
Make
stripes
with
different
pairs of
threads.

Try making
stripes with
three threads
at once. This
is a bit tricky
but looks
good. Keep
the threads in
sequence
carefully.

14

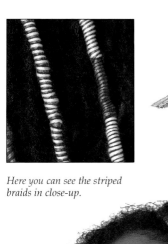

Here you can see the striped braids in close-up.

This thick, stripy braid looks nice down the back of her head.

Several striped braids look stunning together.

Criss-cross

This is another "on top" pattern like the spiral on pages 12-13. It is just as easy to do and looks even more decorative. Always try to make your diagonal, on top winding as neat and evenly-spaced as possible. You will improve with practice.

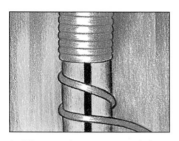

1. The simplest variety of this pattern is with two shades of thread. Tie them to the hair and start braiding with one thread, binding the other thread in. Bind for at least 5cm (2in)

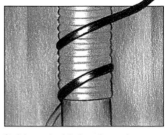

2. Now, hold the thread you were binding with against the strand of hair. Wind the other thread diagonally up around the braid a few times. Try to space the diagonal turns widely and evenly.

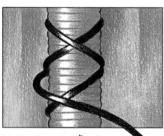

3. At the top (or earlier, if you like), wind the thread back down around the braid again, criss-crossing the diagonals you made on the way up. Adjust the thread with your fingers to make it lie as you want it to.

4. When you get back to where you were, carry on binding using any pattern you like. You could carry on winding with the thread you just used to make the criss-cross pattern; or, alternatively, bind that thread in and continue with the other one.

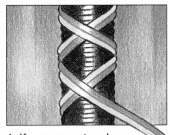

5. Repeat the criss-cross as many times as you like down the braid, with either thread. Finish off with a tight knot.

6. If you are using three or more different threads, try criss-crossing with two at the same time.

This double criss-cross is very effective over black thread.

Make sure both criss-cross threads lie flat against the braid at each turn.

Beads on the end

You can decorate your braids even more by adding beads. You can buy beads which don't cost very much from craft suppliers, or use beads from a broken necklace.

The braid above has a felt bead on the end. It is soft and light and comfortable to wear.

These are paper and clay beads. The braid shows many different patterns.

1. Braid the strand of hair, using any patterns you like, in the normal way. Tie the threads in a tight knot when you reach the end.

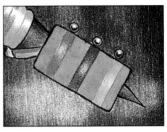

2. Push all the threads and the hair through the hole in one or more beads (the hole must be fairly big). Wet the hair if you can't get it through.

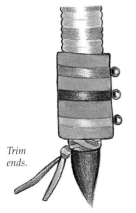

Use thread from the braid if there's enough left, or tie on more.

Trim ends.

3. Wind thread around on top of itself to make a bulky lump below the bead. Tie a knot.

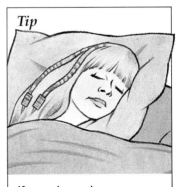

Tip

If you plan to keep your braid in for a long time, remember that beads could be a little uncomfortable to sleep on. Use light beads that are not too big if you can.

Beads all the way

In this bead variation you use tiny glass beads. They don't cost much and they look extra pretty for a special occasion. Use shiny thread, too, for a party look.

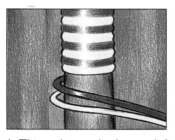

1. This technique looks good if you use one shade of thread only, and contrasting tiny beads. Start to bind the hair.

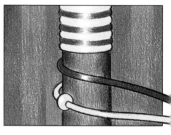

2. Whenever you like, slip a bead onto the thread, push it up against the braid and start winding again tightly below it.

Make sure the beads have big enough holes for the thread.

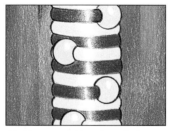

Using all the same beads looks good, but a mixture of beads is fun, too.

3. Continue like this all down the braid. Try to put the beads on at fairly regular intervals. Move them with your fingers so that they lie on different sides of the braid.

Most craft stores have a selection of beads.

Here, beads have been used on a striped braid. Slip the bead onto one strand of thread only and continue winding.

Co-ordinate your braid and beads with your outfit. They can look stunning peeking out from under a hat.

You need small beads to thread on a braid like this but they must have holes big enough to pass the thread through.

Extensions

You can make your braid extra long so that it hangs down below the rest of your hair. This looks eye-catching, especially if you have fairly short hair. Here are some ways to add extensions.

Thread extension

1. Wind a braid using several threads - you need at least six to make this work. Wind tightly right to the end of the strand of hair.

2. Now start to wind with one thread only around all the other threads. Change threads as often as you like.

3. Continue winding to the length you want. Tie all the threads in a tight double knot. Trim the ends to make them equal.

This picture shows a thread extension. Leave the ends fairly long to make a tassel, if you like.

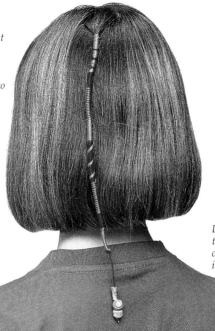

This is a different kind of braid extension, made with a leather thong. See how to do it below.

The beads must have big enough holes for the thong to pass through. Test them before you start.

Don't make the thong too long or it might get in your way.

Thong extension

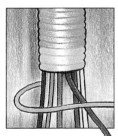

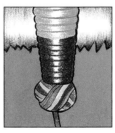

1. From about three-quarters down the braid, bind in a leather thong, thin ribbon or other long, thin string.

2. Bind to the end of the hair and then on around the thong a short way. Tie the threads in a knot around the thong and trim the ends.

3. Cut the thong to the length you want. Thread one or more beads onto the end and tie a double knot tightly below.

23

Unusual braids

You can find all kinds of things to wind around your hair and decorate your braids with. Sometimes you may feel like doing something a little unusual. You need to remember that some things are not suitable to wash so they cannot be left in when you wash your hair, but they can be worth doing for just a few days for a change.

Knitting yarn braids

Bind a braid using knitting yarns. They come in all kinds of thicknesses and textures. Try mixing knobbly ones, thick ones and glittery ones.

This works best on very thick or wiry hair, as the yarn is too bulky for fine hair. It's not a good idea to wash a knitting yarn braid.

This yarn changes shade every few twists so you get a rainbow-effect braid with only one wound strand.

A summertime braid

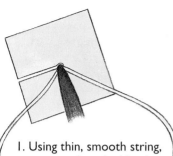

1. Using thin, smooth string, measure, then double, the amount you need and cut. Tie the middle around a thick strand of hair.

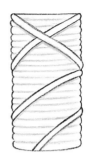

2. Bind tightly in the normal way. Do patterns on top of the braid with one of the lengths of string. Don't wash this braid.

Add flowers or seeds to the braid to decorate it. This braid has poppy heads painted gold tied to it with thread.

String will not stay in very fine, slippery hair very well.

Braid styles

Now you can do all kinds of braids, try combining them in a hairstyle as a pretty feature. There are some ideas to inspire you on the next six pages.

Hairband

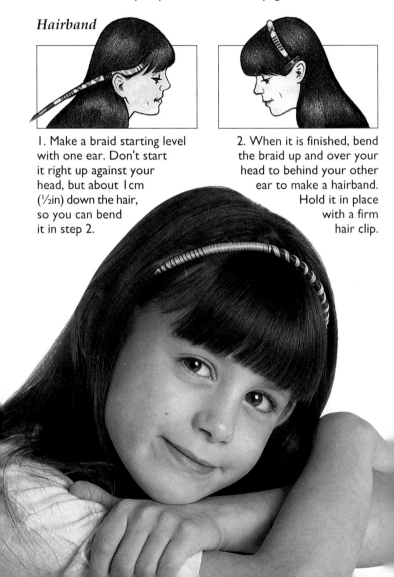

1. Make a braid starting level with one ear. Don't start it right up against your head, but about 1cm (½in) down the hair, so you can bend it in step 2.

2. When it is finished, bend the braid up and over your head to behind your other ear to make a hairband. Hold it in place with a firm hair clip.

Joined braids

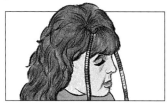

1. Bind a braid on either side of a middle parting, right at the front of your head. Trim the ends of the threads on one braid, but leave them long on the other.

2. Brush the loose hair, then bring both braids fairly loosely over the hair to meet at the back. Bind the long threads around both braids to join them. Tie a knot.

Braid and plait

There are all sorts of ways to combine braids with plaited hair. Here are just a few suggestions.

Alternating braid

1. Bind a strand of hair for a short distance, then tie the threads in a knot and trim. Divide the hair into three thin strands and plait neatly (see page 31 for plaiting reminders).

2. After whatever distance you like, knot the threads together again and tie them back on. Bind the strand once more. Repeat as many times as you like down the hair.

This braid combines the two ideas on these pages. The hair is braided with three threads for a short distance, then the hair is plaited, with one thread along each strand of the plait, then the hair is bound again.

Three-strand plait

1. Tie three threads around a strand of hair. Tie them in a bow at the top. Divide the hair into three and lay a thread along each part.

2. Plait the hair with the threads. Make sure the threads are on top of the hair at each turn, so you can see them.

Above you can see the braid and plait ideas close-up.

The hair is plaited with one strand in each section all the way down this braid.

Use gold and silver glittery threads for a party braid.

More ideas

If you keep a braid in for several days, or even weeks, you may want to tie your hair back out of the way sometimes. All you need to do is fasten the braid up with the hair, as shown here.

Bind a fairly fat braid.

This stripy braid at the back of the head, shown on page 15, has been plaited loosely into the middle strand of a single plait (see how to plait opposite).

Here, three braids have been pulled back into a pony tail. Make sure the braids lie on top of the other hair to show them off.

You can probably think of lots of other ways to show off your braided hair. You and your friends can treat each other to braids whenever you like.

How to plait

Some of the styles in this book involve plaiting your hair. In case you're not an expert, here is the basic method to remind you how to do it.

1. Divide the hair into three equal sections. Hold the right and middle sections in your hands.

2. Cross your hands so the right section comes over the middle section and they swap places, as shown.

3. Hold what is now the right hand section in your thumb and first finger and the middle section in the other fingers.

4. Cross the left section over the middle and take it in your right fingers. Swap the middle section to your left hand.

5. Cross the right section over the middle section again. Swap it to the fingers of your left hand.

It feels awkward at first, but you'll soon get used to it.

6. Keep on like this, crossing the left, then the right side over the middle to the end of the hair. Hold with a band.

Index

First published in 1996 by Usborne Publishing Ltd, Usborne House, 83-85 Saffron Hill,
London EC1N 8RT, England.

Printed in Italy.